THE
OREGON TRAIL
and WESTWARD
EXPANSION

A HISTORY PERSPECTIVES BOOK

Kristin Marciniak

Published in the United States of America by Cherry Lake Publishing
Ann Arbor, Michigan
www.cherrylakepublishing.com

Consultants: Jason LaBau, PhD, U.S. History, Lecturer, California State
Polytechnic University, Pomona; Marla Conn, ReadAbility, Inc.
Editorial direction: Red Line Editorial
Book design and illustration: Sleeping Bear Press

Photo Credits: Library of Congress, cover (left), cover (right), 1 (left), 1
(right), 22; Heyn Photo/Library of Congress, cover (middle), 1 (middle),
12; North Wind/North Wind Picture Archives, 4, 6, 10, 14, 16, 18, 21, 24,
28, 30

Library of Congress Cataloging-in-Publication Data
Marciniak, Kristin.
 The Oregon Trail and westward expansion / Kristin Marciniak.
    pages cm. – (Perspectives library)
  ISBN 978-1-62431-419-3 (hardcover) – ISBN 978-1-62431-495-7 (pbk.)
– ISBN 978-1-62431-457-5 (pdf) – ISBN 978-1-62431-533-6 (ebook)
1. Oregon National Historic Trail–Juvenile literature. 2. Overland journeys
to the Pacific–Juvenile literature. 3. Frontier and pioneer life–West (U.S.)–
Juvenile literature. I. Title.
F597.M34 2013
978'.02–dc23
                                 2013008488

Cherry Lake Publishing would like to acknowledge the work of
The Partnership for 21st Century Skills. Please visit *www.p21.org*
for more information.

Printed in the United States of America
Corporate Graphics Inc.
July 2013
CLFA11

TABLE OF CONTENTS

In this book, you will read about the Oregon Trail and westward expansion from three perspectives. Each perspective is based on real things that happened to real people who traveled or experienced the Oregon Trail. As you'll see, the same event can look different depending on one's point of view.

1

Abigail Petersen
Pioneer

A letter from my husband's brother William changed our lives. "Pack your things and kiss your mother goodbye, Abigail. We're going West!" David whooped as he handed me the letter.

A year ago, William left our **rural** Illinois community with a group headed toward the untamed land west of the Mississippi River. He hoped for good soil and mild winters, neither of which we had at home. Times have been tough for the past few years. We all wanted a new beginning and eagerly latched on to the idea of expanding the United States all the way west.

William found what he was looking for in Oregon Country. He claimed land in the Willamette Valley, at the very end of the Oregon Trail. Now he was sending for his wife, Elspeth, and their three children. David decided we were up for the adventure too. Within a month, we purchased supplies, sold our farm and most of our belongings, and headed toward the beginning of the trail in Independence, Missouri.

Our family was just one of hundreds that gathered in Independence in May 1843. It was later called the Great Migration of 1843. Altogether, we had 1,000 people, 120 wagons, and nearly 5,000 head of cattle as we started the 2,000-mile trek to Oregon Country. We hoped the journey would only take five months. We wanted to pass through the mountains before snow started to fall.

The oxen pulling the wagons were strong but slow, and we traveled just ten to 12 miles each day. Horses, while faster, wouldn't have been able to pull our supplies. Our wagon carried all of the **staples** we'd need for the next few months—flour, sugar, coffee, rice, and bacon. I brought my trusty cast-iron skillet for cooking over the nightly campfire. Hunting supplies, bedding, candles, and tools were all packed

Wagons were packed full with supplies for the long journey. ▶

tightly into our **prairie schooner**. We also had to bring food for the animals, so we hauled bags of grain. David guessed that the wagon weighed more than one ton once it was all packed. Not an inch of space was wasted, but the heavy load meant that we had to walk most of the time.

THINK ABOUT IT

▶ Read this paragraph closely. What is its main point? Cite specific evidence from the text to support your answer.

At night, we formed the wagons into a giant circle with all the livestock in the middle. The wagons served as a **stockade**, keeping the animals from escaping into the wilderness. Once protected by the circled wagons, we started preparing to bed down for the night. David and Billy, Elspeth's son, unhitched the oxen and took care of the rest of the animals. The smaller children collected firewood. Elspeth and I found a stream nearby where we gathered water for washing and drinking. Then we began preparing dinner. After dinner, we washed dishes and prepared lunch for the next day. While we slept under the sky, some of the men took turns looking out for Indians. We had all heard stories of wild Indian tribes attacking wagon trains, but, thankfully, we never encountered any. The next morning, I'd have breakfast ready for David before he fed the animals at 4:00 a.m., and we'd be back on the trail before the sun rose.

MANIFEST DESTINY

Manifest Destiny was the term politicians and leaders used to explain why the United States was meant to spread across the entire North American continent. It meant the country was destined to expand to the west. John O'Sullivan first used the phrase in July 1845 in an article published in the *United States Magazine and Democratic Review*.

The trip was grueling, and many in our party fell ill along the way. About halfway through the trip, Billy got sick. We had just gone through the South Pass, a large area of open prairie that separates the Rocky Mountains, when Billy began vomiting clear liquid. He had a fever and a thirst that could not be satisfied. It was **cholera**, and the poor boy was dead within a few days. Back in Illinois, we had heard that the West was healthier for our families, the fresh air curing everything from smallpox to influenza. But many people in our group never made it to Oregon Country to find out.

Some died from illness, and others died in accidents. People fell under wagon wheels, drowned during river crossings, or were trampled by their own animals. In all, we lost nearly 100 people between Independence and the Willamette Valley. We didn't have wood to build coffins, so most families wrapped their lost relatives in blankets and buried them

Crossing rivers on the Oregon Trail could be dangerous. ▶

under the trail. It seems harsh now, but we didn't want wild animals to pick up the scent of the bodies. The rolling wagon wheels packed down the dirt and we continued west.

The last part of the trip was the hardest. Not only were we heartbroken over Billy's death, but we still had to cross the Blue Mountains and the Cascade Mountains. The weather was growing colder, and we were running out of supplies. The animals couldn't move quickly on the mountain terrain, and our already-slow pace became a crawl. Some people lightened their load by completely abandoning their wagons at Fort Hall, just inside Oregon Country. The only supplies they had for the next 900 miles were those they could carry.

Once we reached The Dalles, a city near the end of our journey, we had to face the deadly rapids of the Columbia River. Floating down the river was dangerous, but it was the only way to get to the Willamette Valley. We had come too far to give up now. David and a few other men took the wheels off our wagon and turned it into a makeshift boat. Those without wagons felled trees and built flat-bottomed rafts. In the middle of October 1843, soaking wet and freezing, we finally arrived in the Willamette Valley. Our travels had ended, but our adventure was just beginning.

SECOND SOURCE

▶ Find an outside source that describes life along the Oregon Trail. Compare the information from your source to the information here. How are they alike? How are they different?

2

Kuckunniwi

Cheyenne Tribesman

I was just a boy of 11 in 1843, when the first large group of settlers crossed our summer hunting grounds. All ten bands, or family groups, of Cheyenne people had gathered to hunt buffalo and smaller game along the path taken by the white men traveling to Oregon Country. I was excited by these new visitors—but also afraid. They looked and acted so different from us.

I had never seen a white man before. My brothers and sisters hadn't either. But our father remembered the **missionaries** from the 1830s. They were kind at first, he said. Cheyenne elders thought they could live in peace with these new neighbors. But by the time they realized their mistake, it was too late. The white man, my father explained, wanted to change our way of life by forcing us to become part of their society.

We watched the wagon train leave our hunting grounds, moving toward the Rocky Mountains. I thought that was the last I would see of the white man. I was wrong.

It is 1852, and I am 20 now. Like the rest of the men in my band, I spend the days hunting. Buffalo is our main source of food, clothing, and shelter. We hunt on horseback using bows and arrows to shoot the buffalo. Sometimes we drive the herd off cliffs or into deep snow. We hunt other large animals, including deer and wild sheep, and smaller animals such as coyotes, foxes, and rabbits.

We Cheyenne are **nomads**. We follow the buffalo across the open plains. During the winter months, each band follows a different group of buffalo. In the summer, when the buffalo gather in one place,

▲ *Many plains tribes relied on the buffalo for food, shelter, and clothing.*

the entire tribe comes together for hunting and tribal ceremonies.

We do not have permanent homes. When the buffalo move to a new location, the women pack up our camp so we can follow. Women own and take care of our three-poled teepees, which are draped in buffalo skins. The women are in charge of finding water and firewood, cooking, and making all the clothing and ceremonial robes. Men hunt and fight when necessary. Every person in our band has a responsibility, right down to the small boys who tend the horses.

Horses are an important part of Cheyenne life. Our band of 300 people has a herd of 1,000. We ride them to chase the buffalo. We raise them for trade with other tribes and the white man. While we try to live off the land as much as possible, there are some things we cannot make. We must purchase or **barter** for guns, ammunition, knives, kettles, cloth, and glass beads.

▲ *The Cheyenne met with white settlers to purchase or barter for goods they could not make.*

We depend on the white man for these items, but it is an uneasy relationship. The white man fears us and calls us uncivilized savages. He does not understand that people can live differently, and that we have thrived this way for hundreds of years. He only sees wide-open land that is free for his taking and thinks we are standing in his way.

Just as he fears us, we fear him. Not only because he has weapons. Our bows and arrows are faster and just as deadly as their guns. It is the power that he holds over us that frightens us. As more settlers move to the West, our land is getting smaller. We, along with many other tribes, have entered **treaties** with the U.S. government in efforts to protect our people and way of life. In exchange, we are often forced to give up the land we have roamed for years.

Such a treaty was signed last year, in 1851. Cheyenne leaders, as well as elders from the Arapaho, Teton Sioux, and Crow tribes, met with U.S. officials at Fort Laramie. Each tribe was assigned to a specific area of the plains. In exchange, we would receive protection from hostile settlers and $50,000

▲ *Treaties between the U.S. government and Native Americans often took land away from tribes.*

in supplies. The Cheyenne and Arapaho people are now limited to land between the Platte River and the Arkansas River, west of the Rocky Mountain foothills.

The buffalo are still free to roam, but we are not. The herds are thinning because the white man hunts them for food and sport. We are not allowed to leave our land to follow those that are left. I often wonder what is to become of my people if the buffalo disappear. How will we feed, clothe, and shelter our families? How will we survive?

The numbers of Cheyenne are already growing smaller. Since the white man began steadily crossing our land nine years ago, he has brought diseases that we have never before seen. These include smallpox and

TREATIES

Treaties between the United States and Native Americans resulted in the United States taking more and more land away from the Native Americans. Just a few years after the treaty at Fort Laramie, the Kansas-Nebraska Act of 1854 took land from Indian Territory to create the states of Kansas and Nebraska.

black measles. Two entire bands of Cheyenne were killed by cholera in 1849. A third was so badly affected that the survivors had to join another band. Many in my band became ill, but fortunately most survived. I fear we do not have much to look forward to though.

Last year, the white man's Congress created a policy that forces native people to live on reservations, away from the trails and new settlements. My people have been spared so far, but I have heard of other plains peoples who have already been moved. Unable to hunt the buffalo, they are starving. The government promises them supplies, but the supplies either never show up or are stolen by thieves to sell for profit. It is a grim life. I don't know what will happen to us, but I cannot bear the thought of my people meeting such a fate.

SECOND SOURCE

▶ What is the main point of this chapter? Identify two pieces of evidence that support this idea.

▲ *Native American tribes were forced to move from their land to reservations.*

3

Charles Mills

Soldier at Fort Laramie

I envy the folks who pass through Fort Laramie, where I'm stationed. They come through on foot and by wagon so they can start a new life in this unclaimed territory. I've never been farther west than a few miles past Fort Laramie. But once my time here is finished, I'm going home to Iowa to marry Betsy. Then we'll come back to the West to start our new life together.

For now, though, Fort Laramie is a fine place to be. It's right in the middle of the Oregon Trail, and we also see our fair share of folks headed out to California for gold. Set on the banks of the Laramie and the North Platte Rivers, we give people a place to gossip, stock up on supplies, and take a much-needed rest during their travels.

The fort hasn't always been called Laramie, but it has been a gathering place for adventurous travelers since 1834. That's when the fur traders built a trading post out of logs and called it Fort William. The log buildings didn't last long, so the fort was rebuilt out of adobe bricks in 1841 and renamed Fort John. Soon the big wagon trains started passing by, and the fort became the only place to stock up on supplies for 800 miles.

Then the forty-niners came. It was gold fever out there in California, and the government decided that the West needed a stronger military presence to protect the travelers. So they bought many of the forts along the trail. They renamed this one Fort Laramie, and the name remains the same today, in 1860.

Protection is our first job here. We make sure the travelers feel safe on their travels, and the trails are clear for wagons and livestock. Settlers can buy supplies like animal feed, tea, flour, and even ammunition. They can have a broken wagon axle

▲ *Fort Laramie was a useful stop for pioneers on the Oregon Trail.*

fixed or replace a bent wheel. If someone in their party is sick, they can stay for a few days or send messages to folks back home who may be worrying about them. But most folks who stop at the fort just want information about the trail ahead.

A lot of people who come through these parts are afraid of the Indians. I've been here for two years and haven't come up against any troubles, but I know there have been some problems in the past. For the most part, the Plains Indians keep their distance from the settlers. We do get reports of stolen horses, and sometimes a tribe will ask a wagon train for payment to cross their land. There's not much we can do about that if we want to keep the peace.

SECOND SOURCE

▶ Find another source about Fort Laramie or other forts along the Oregon Trail. Compare the information from that source to the information in this chapter. How is it similar? How is it different?

The situation with the Indians is delicate. We've been lucky here at Fort Laramie—the last time fighting broke out here was six years ago. It was just a few miles from the fort back in 1854. A cow from a passing wagon train wandered into a Sioux village. The Sioux were hungry, and they were waiting for their shipment of supplies from the government. One of the tribesmen killed the cow for meat. People from the wagon train came up to the fort to complain, and Lieutenant Grattan and 28 other soldiers went to arrest the Indian. Things got bad. The chief of the tribe was killed, as were all the Americans.

The old-timers tell me the relationship between the Indians and Americans has been rocky ever since. The settlers want to expand the United States westward, and the Indians want the land that was given to them in the treaties. Recently, there's been a lot of fighting over the land near Pikes Peak in the Rocky Mountains. Gold was found in Pikes Peak in 1858, and now miners are crawling all over the place, trespassing on Indian lands. I know it doesn't sound right, me being a soldier and all, but I sometimes feel bad for the Indians. At the end of the day, we all just want to live on this beautiful land.

That's what I'm planning to do when my time at the fort is done. I've been stationed here for two years already, and I suppose I'll be here for two more unless things get worse back East. Betsy sent word that states in the South want to **secede** from our country to start their own. Many people from the North do not want slavery in new lands, while many in the South think it is necessary for their economy. I'll fight for the North if I'm called home, but I hope the sides can settle their differences without

▲ *People trespassed on Native American lands after gold was found in the West.*

bloodshed. This is a great big country, and it keeps getting bigger every day. Surely we can all find space to live our lives the way we want.

END OF THE TRAIL

The Oregon Trail was heavily traveled until 1884, when Union Pacific completed a railroad along the same route. After that, it was much faster and less expensive to travel to the West by rail. The trail was still used to move cattle for many years.

LOOK, LOOK AGAIN

Closely examine this image of a wagon train on the Oregon Trail. Answer the following questions:

1. How would a pioneer describe this scene in a letter to family back East?

2. How would a Cheyenne tribesman from the Great Plains react to this picture?

3. What concerns might a soldier at a military fort have after seeing this image?

GLOSSARY

barter (BAHR-tur) to exchange things for other things rather than using money

cholera (KAH-lur-uh) a serious disease that causes severe vomiting and diarrhea and often results in death

missionary (MISH-uh-ner-ee) a person who is sent to a foreign land to teach about religion and do religious work

nomad (NOH-mad) a member of a group of people who move from place to place instead of living in one place all the time

prairie schooner (PRAIR-ee SKOO-nur) a large covered wagon used by the pioneers to move west

rural (ROOR-uhl) relating to the country, rather than the city, and the people who live there

secede (si-SEED) to formally leave a group, such as the Union

staple (STAY-puhl) an important supply, such as food, that is used very often

stockade (stah-KADE) a barrier that is used to defend a place

treaty (TREE-tee) an official agreement that is made between two or more countries or groups

LEARN MORE

Further Reading

Domnauer, Teresa. *Westward Expansion*. New York: Children's Press, 2010.
Friedman, Mel. *The Oregon Trail*. New York: Children's Press, 2013.
Roza, Greg. *Westward Expansion*. New York: Gareth Stevens, 2011.

Web Sites

End of the Oregon Trail: Historic Oregon City
http://www.historicoregoncity.org/index.php/widgetkit/oregon-trail-history/item/
   trails-faqs?category_id=6
This Web site has information on the history of the Oregon Trail, as well as pioneer families who traveled the trail.

National Historical Oregon Trail Interpretive Center
http://www.blm.gov/or/oregontrail
On this Web site, readers can learn more about the Oregon Trail and discover what life was like for kids who traveled on it.

INDEX

ABOUT THE AUTHOR

Kristin Marciniak grew up in Bettendorf, Iowa, and now lives in Kansas City, Missouri. She has a bachelor's degree of journalism from the University of Missouri–Columbia. When she's not writing about key moments in American history, she likes to read, sew, knit, and spend time with her son and husband.